CW01582558

Londo
Colour
Book

Look out for the fun London 2012 facts throughout this book!

Find the right sticker for each fact and stick it in place.

First published 2011 under license by Carlton Books Limited

Carlton Books Limited
20 Mortimer Street, London W1T 3JW
Created for Carlton by SkyJack Publishing Limited
ISBN 978-1-84732-897-7

Printed in China

A CIP catalogue record for this book is available from the British Library.

MIX
Paper from responsible sources
FSC® C101537

Please remember to recycle this book when you have finished enjoying it.

Welcome!

Meet the official mascots of the London 2012 Olympic and Paralympic Games! Wenlock is the Olympic Games mascot and Mandeville is the Paralympic Games mascot.

Colour them in using your brightest pens.

Look at your stickers to see which colours to use, then add some stars to the page.

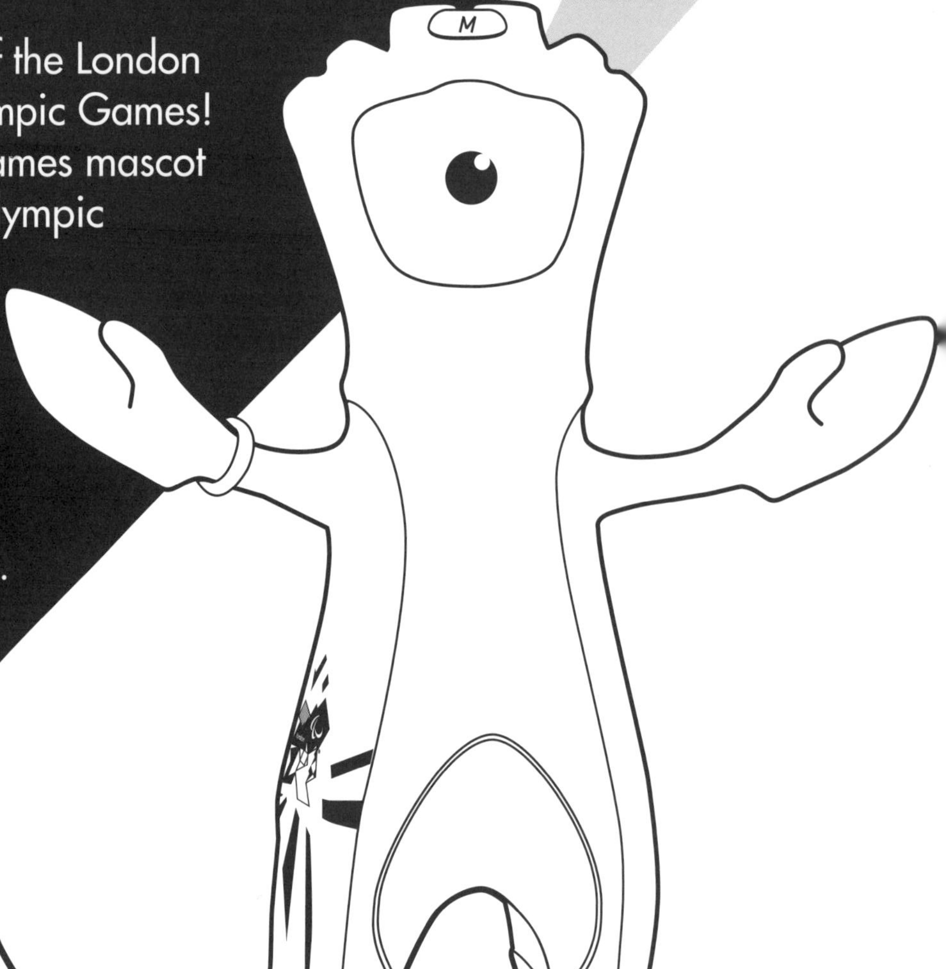

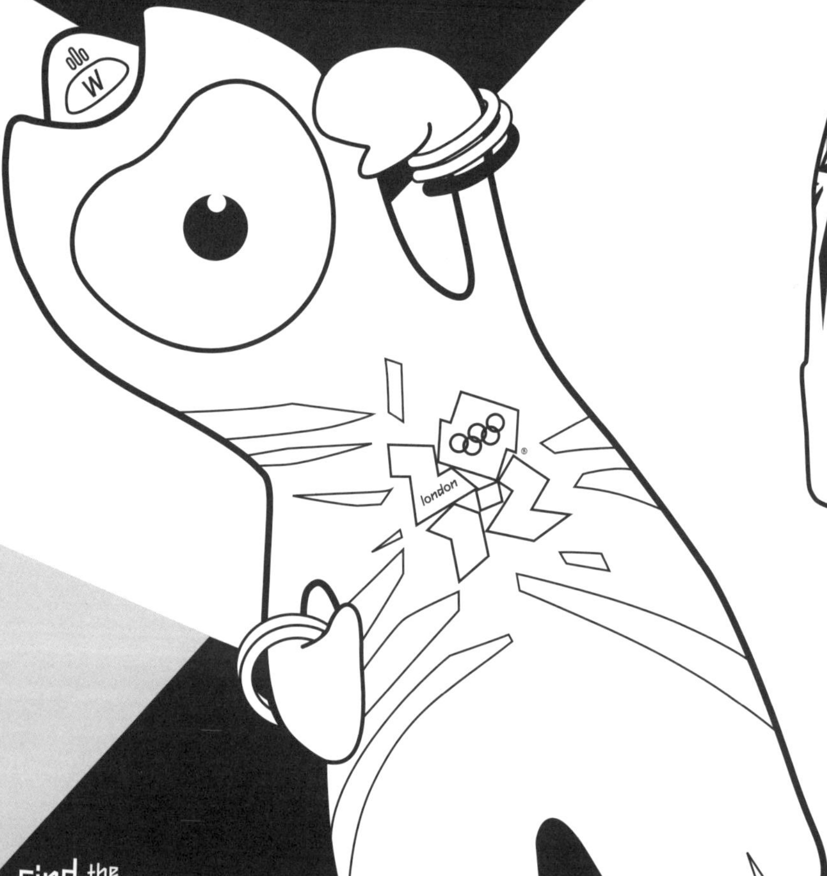

Find the sticker!

Made from the last two drops of steel used for the London 2012 Olympic Stadium, Wenlock and Mandeville are shiny, happy mascots who love to learn about new sports.

On your marks!

Wenlock is ready to race!

Colour him in as quickly as you can.

Use a stopwatch to time how long it takes you, then write your time in the box.

Your Time:

__ __ : __ __

Find the sticker!

Athletics is one of the biggest sports that will feature at the London 2012 Games. You'll see 2,000 athletes running, walking, jumping and throwing for gold!

Flag parade

All these countries have teams competing at London 2012!

Can you colour in their flags? The numbers below tell you which colours to use.

Colour code

1 = red

2 = blue

3 = yellow

4 = green

5 = black

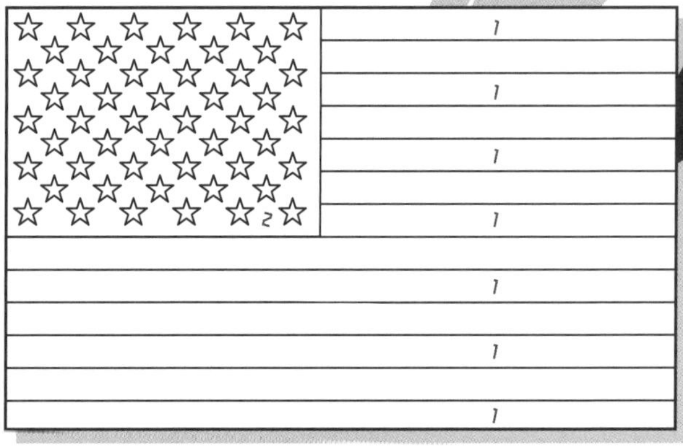

USA

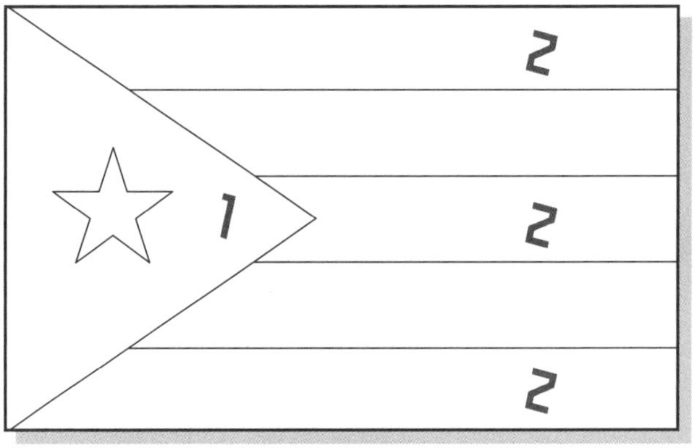

Cuba

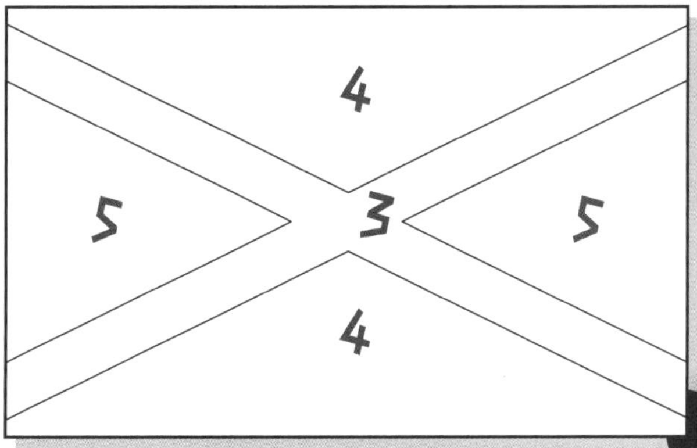

Jamaica

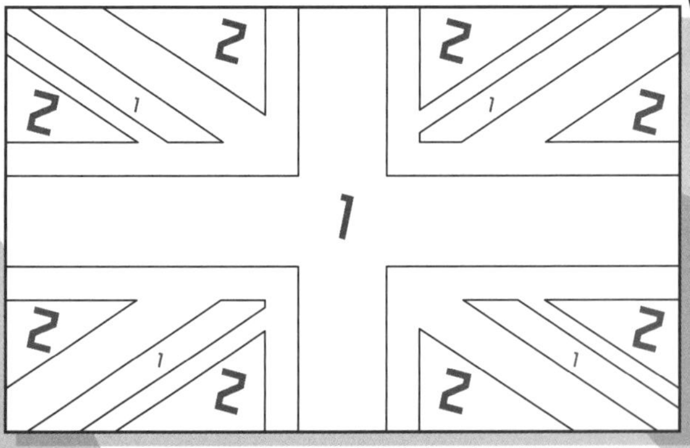

Great Britain

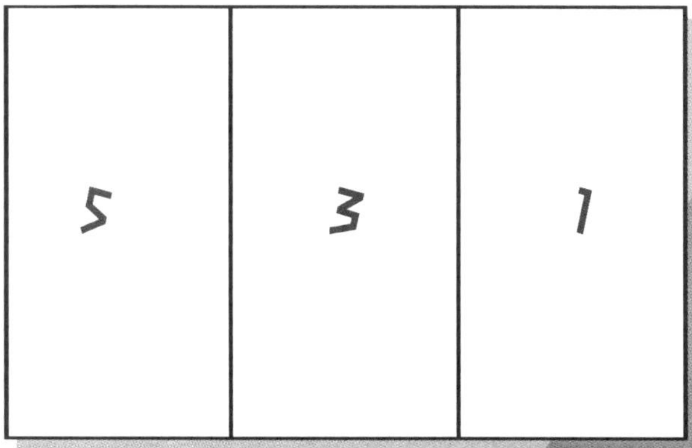

Belgium

Canada

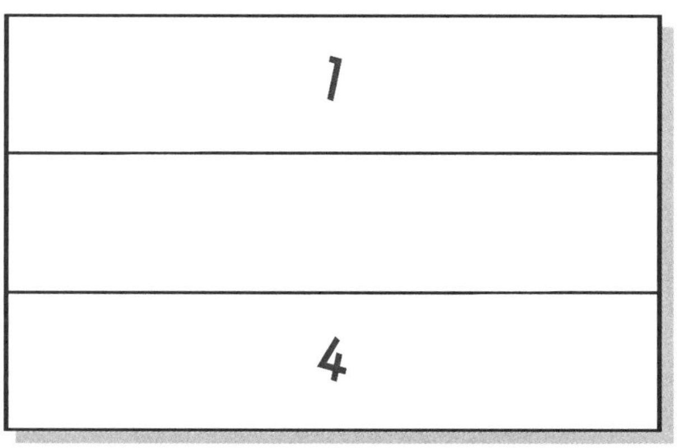

Hungary

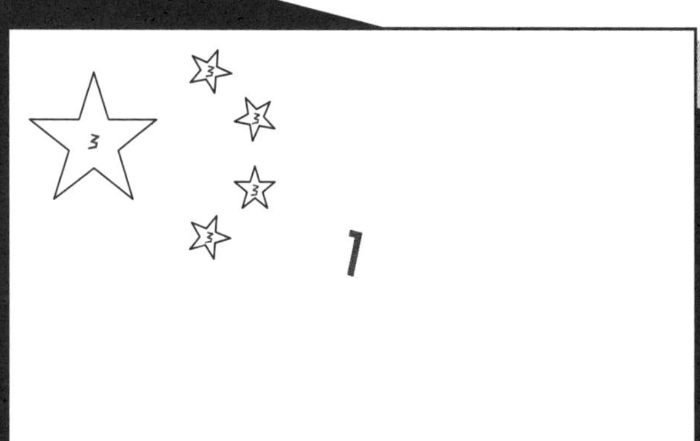

China

Mandeville is supporting British athletes at the Games. Find the sticker of the Union Flag and stick it in place.

Colour in Mandeville too!

Find the sticker!

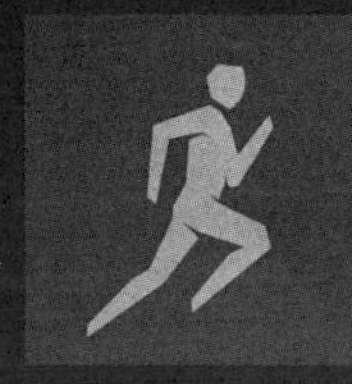

The Opening Ceremony to the Games will take place on July 26th 2012. Flag-bearers for over 200 countries will lead their teams into the Olympic Stadium!

Make a splash!

Swimming is a sport that anyone can try, so why not take a dip in your local pool?

Colour in Wenlock making a splash.

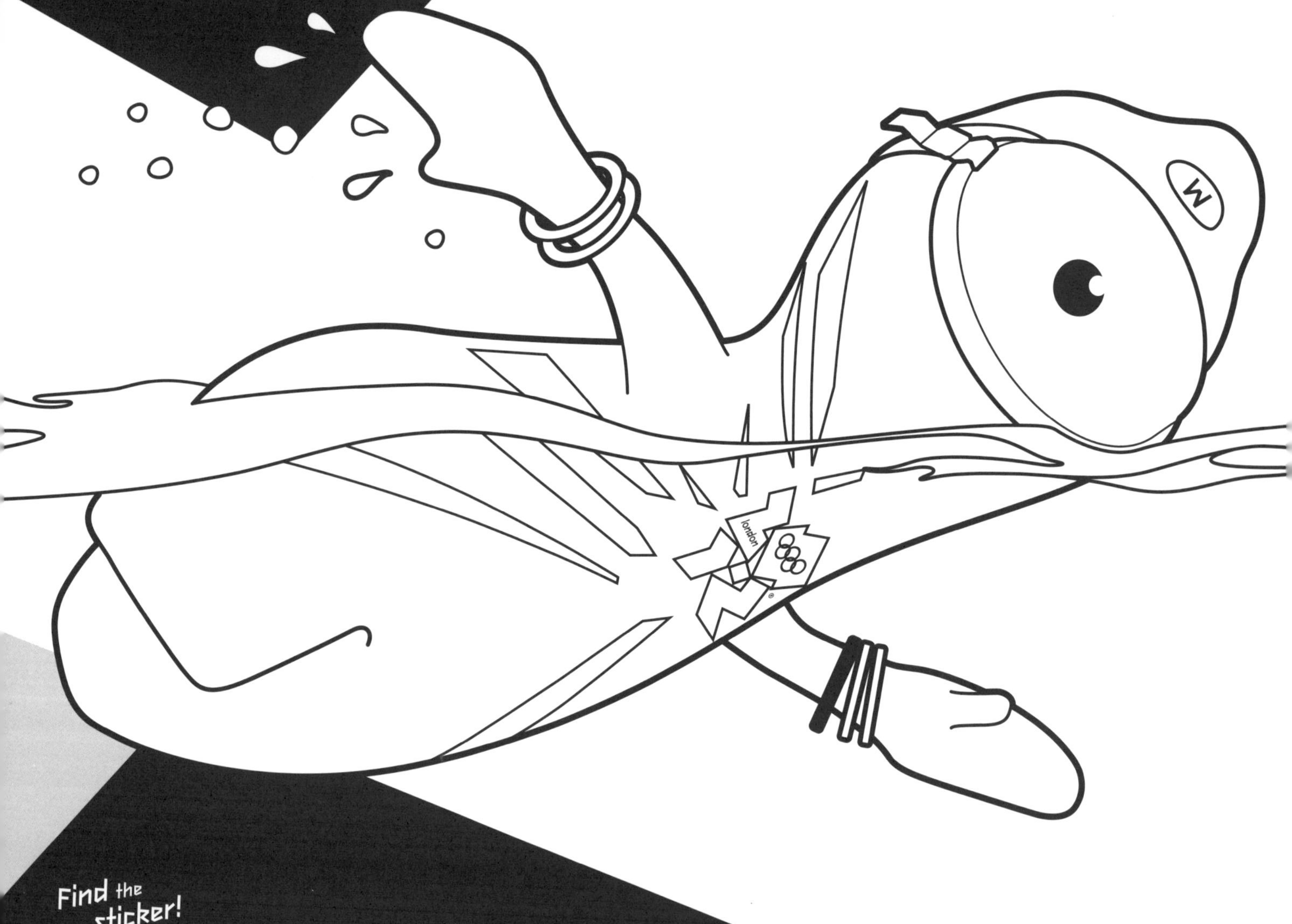

Find the sticker!

Most Swimming races at London 2012 will take place indoors at the Aquatics Centre. Only the tough 10km Marathon swim is held outside.

Be the best

Both Wenlock and Mandeville are sports mad! They want to do their best in as many sports as they can.

Colour the first box if you like playing the sport and colour the second box if you like watching the sport, on TV or live!

	playing	watching
Swimming		
Cycling		
BMX Racing		
Athletics		
Football		
Table Tennis		
Gymnastics		
Equestrian		
Judo		

Find the sticker!

Did you know that Wenlock wears five friendship bands in the colours of the five Olympic rings? And the light on his head is inspired by the lights on London's famous black taxi cabs!

On the ball!

Mandeville loves to play Football – it's his favourite sport! It helps him stay fit and healthy, too.

Colour in Mandeville dribbling with the ball and find the sticker to match your picture!

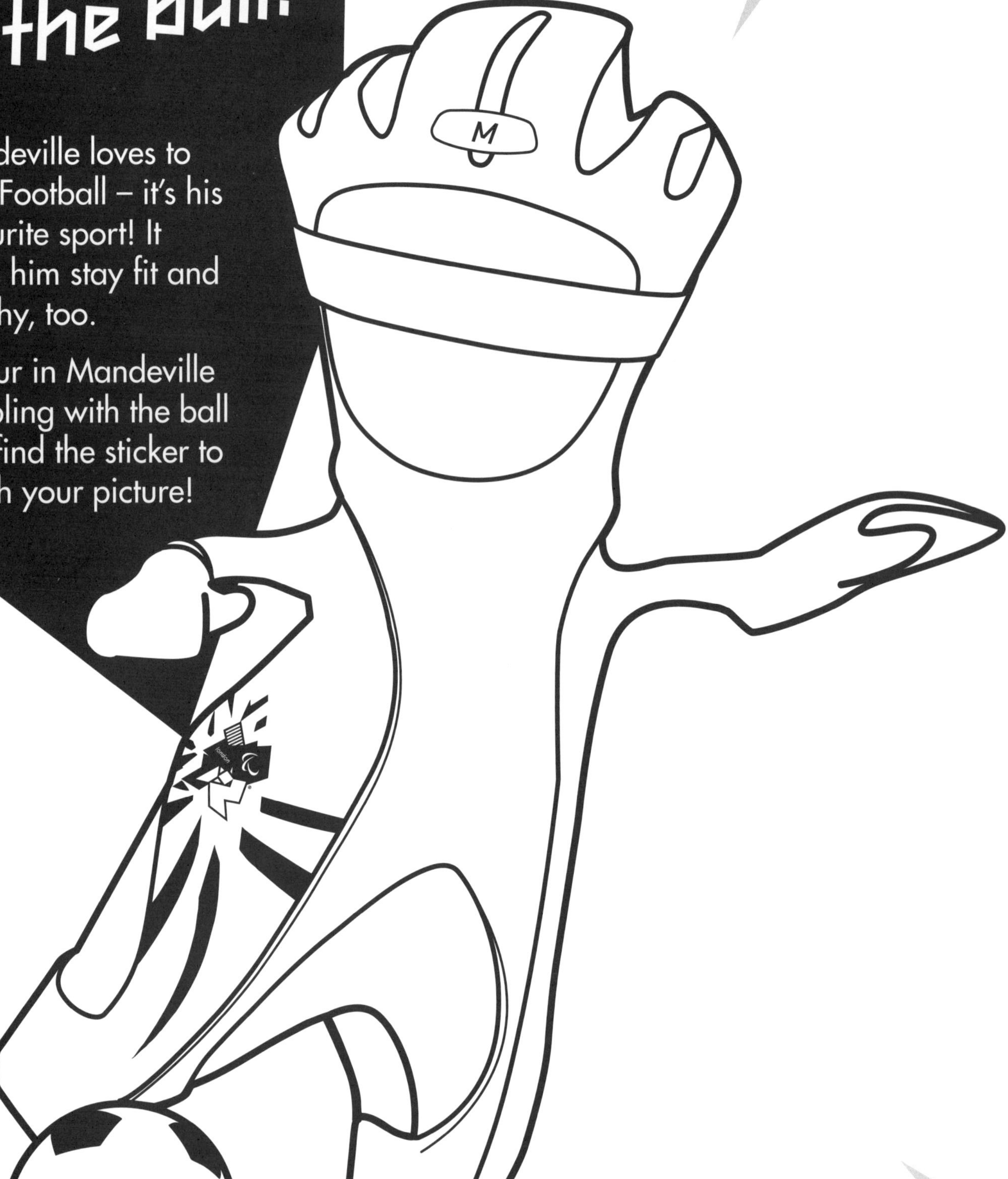

Find the sticker!

The Olympic and Paralympic Football finals will be played at the famous Wembley Stadium.

Move it!

These pictures of Wenlock on the move may look alike, but only two Wenlocks are exactly the same.

Which two make a perfect pair?

a.

b.

c.

d.

e.

f.

Answer: pictures a and f are exactly the same.

Fly the flag!

Mandeville is flying the flag for London 2012! He can't wait for the Games to begin!

Which two pieces are missing from the picture jigsaw?

Draw them in to complete the puzzle, then colour in the picture.

a.

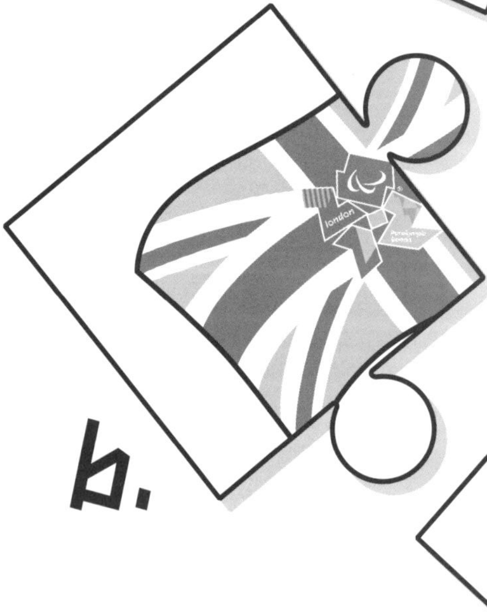

b.

c.

d.

Answer: pieces a and d are missing.

Get sticking!

This time, you'll need three jigsaw piece stickers to complete the picture puzzle.

Stick them in place, then colour in Wenlock the archer!

Find the sticker!

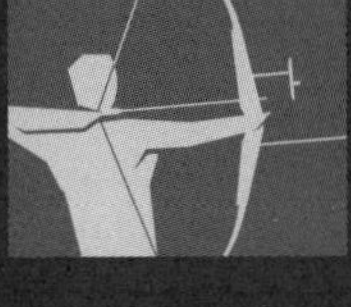

Archery dates back around 10,000 years when bows and arrows were first used for hunting and warfare. It developed into a sport in England in medieval times and first became an Olympic sport at the 1900 Games in Paris.

Colour by numbers

Make Mandeville happy by giving him some colour!

The numbers below tell you which colours to use.

Colour code

1 = blue

2 = grey

3 = orange

4 = pink

5 = green

Find the sticker!

There will be 20 sports at the Paralympic Games, from well-known ones like Swimming and Athletics to more unusual ones like Boccia and Goalball!

Game on!

Wenlock has joined in a Hockey game!

Draw over the lines to complete him dribbling down the wing, then colour in your picture.

Find the sticker!

Hockey gets its name from the French word 'hocquet', meaning 'shepherd's crook'.

R is for ...

Wenlock and Mandeville love to try new sports – they'll give anything a go!

Colour ONLY the pictures of the sports that begin with the letter R, then place your stickers over the sports that are left.

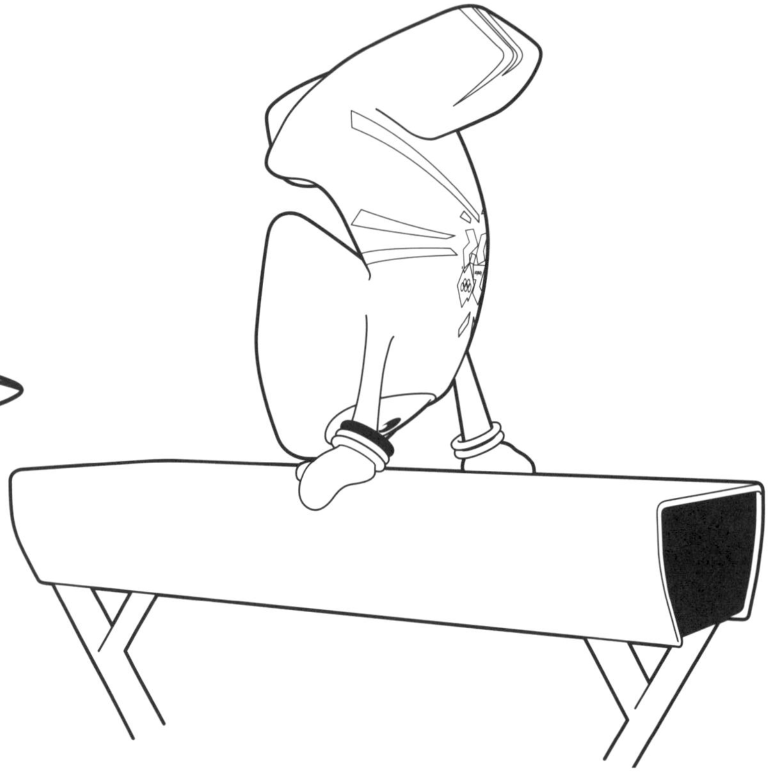

Answer: the sports that begin with R are Rowing and Running.

S is for ...

Now colour ONLY the pictures of the sports that begin with the letter S, and place your stickers over the remaining pictures.

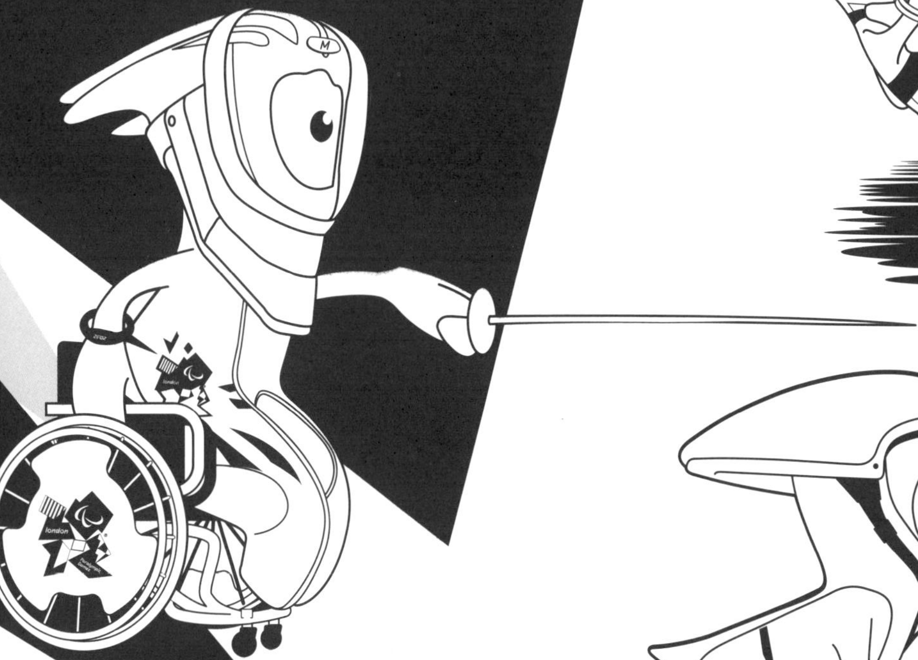

Answer: the sports that begin with S are Swimming and Sailing.

Dot to dot

Starting at number 1, help Mandeville reveal an Olympic surprise.

Then colour the picture in your favourite colours.

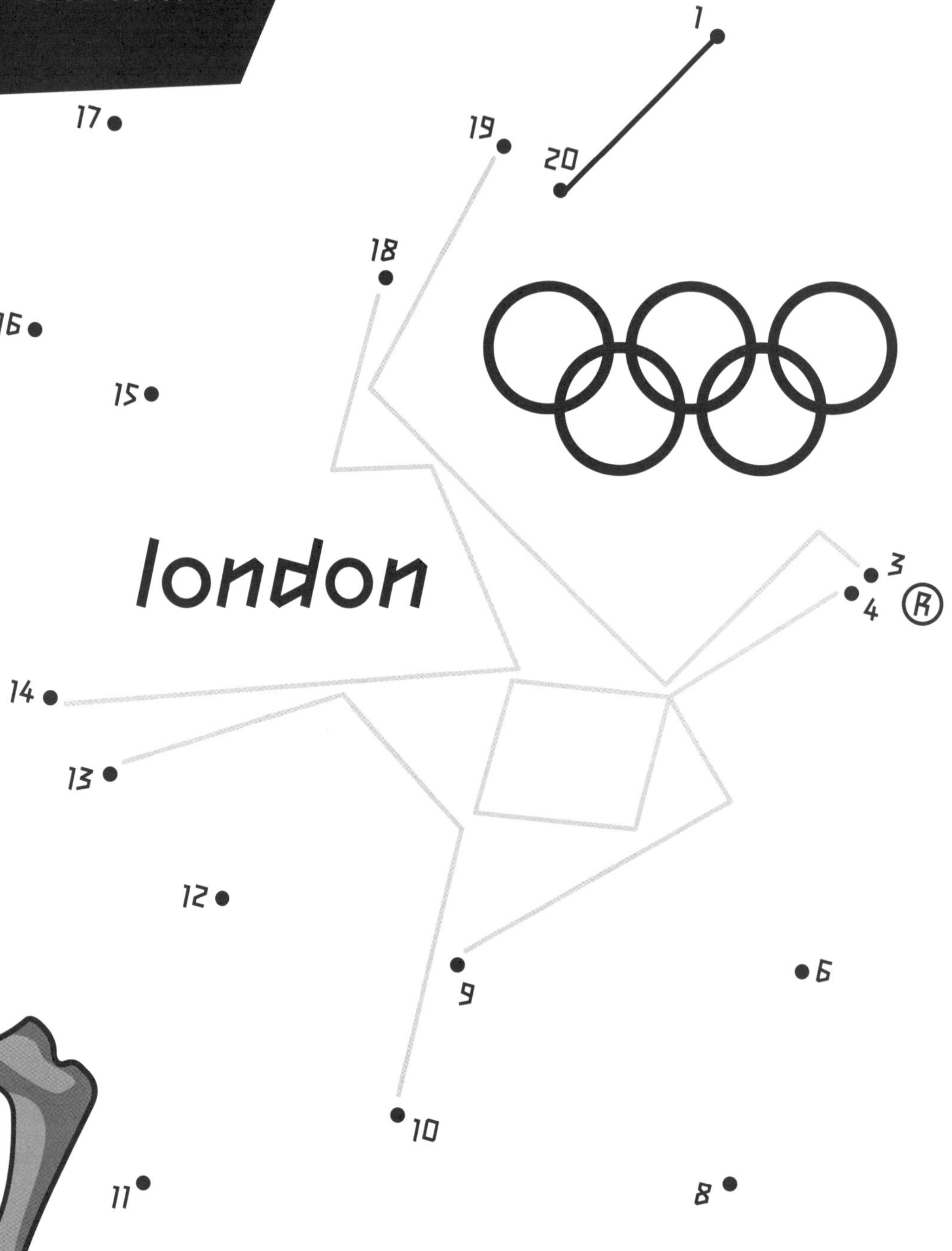

Odd one out

These pictures of Wenlock on the tennis court may look alike, but one is different from the rest.

Can you find the odd one out?

Add a tennis ball sticker when you find it!

a.

b.

c.

d.

e.

f.

Answer: picture f is the odd one out.

Make a match!

Using your stickers, match Mandeville and Wenlock to these sporty shadows!

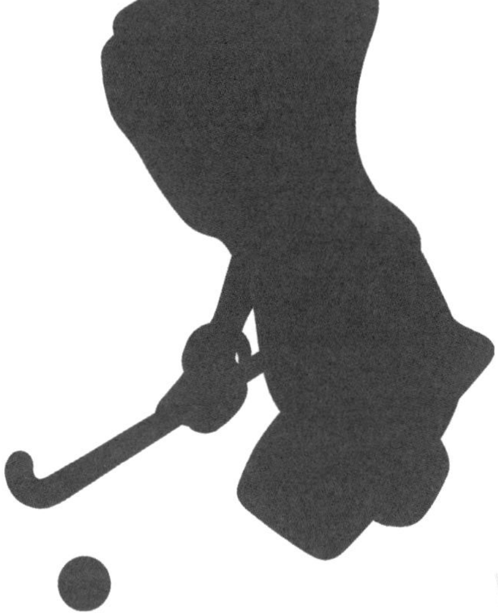

Now look at the stickers and see if you can answer these tricky teasers.

1. Which is the only water sport?

____

2. Which sport can be played as singles or doubles?

____

3. Which sport has eleven players on each side?

____

Answers: 1. Diving, 2. Tennis, 3. Hockey.

Seeing double

Take a look at these two Wenlocks, making waves down on the water!

Can you find 5 differences between the pictures?

1.

2.

Answers: a stripe on the boat is missing, the details on the 1st Wenlock's head are missing and his wristbands have gone, the lines on the 2nd Wenlock's oar have disappeared, the London 2012 emblem is missing.

Sports sketch

Draw over the lines to complete this picture of Wenlock doing his victory dance! Then colour in your picture in Wenlock's favourite colours – red, white and blue.

Going for gold!

Mandeville crosses the finishing line in first place to take the gold medal!

Colour him in using your brightest colours.